Great Expectations

Rising Above the Bog of Singleness

Nicole Sager

Books by Nicole Sager

The Arcrean Conquest
The Heart of Arcrea
The Fate of Arcrea
The Isle of Arcrea

Companions of Arcrea
Hebbros
Burdney

Classic Chats
A Tale of Two Siblings
Great Expectations

Great Expectations: Rising Above the Bog of Singleness
Copyright © 2016 Nicole Sager

Front & Back Cover Photos: ©Nicole Sager

All rights reserved. No part of this book may be reproduced, stored in a retrieval system, or transmitted in any form or by any means—electronic, mechanical, photocopying, recording, or otherwise—without the prior written permission of the copyright owner.

Scripture quotations are from the King James Version of the Bible.

Printed in the United States of America

ISBN-10: 1537578081
ISBN-13: 978-1537578088

*For all of my
Bog Buddies*

CONTENTS

Introduction – Notes From the Quagmire	*1*
I Just Wanna Be Normal!	*6*
A Trial Is a Trial Is a Trial	*13*
Idol Desires	*21*
Making the While Worthwhile	*33*
Joseph & Asenath – A Story of Great Expectations	*39*
In Closing – Build Up, Rise Up	*47*

Introduction
Notes From the Quagmire

Here I sit, encased waist-deep in a thick sticky substance that is all-consuming, unavoidable, and impossible to ignore. This particular quagmire is extensive and inhabited by thousands of poor souls just like me, scattered across this dismal sea of sludge and afraid to look at one another lest a mere glance be misconstrued as something more than accidental eye-contact—lest it be misconstrued as anything at all. It is a bog of great discomfort.

I call it Singleness.

Walking along the banks of this bog are numerous people who look upon us singles with pity; people who once sat among us, but have since linked hands with another and crawled out to dwell within the flowering borders of Marital Bliss. [Yes, the illustration has its shortcomings, but bear with me.] These fine people (even dear friends) offer words of encouragement and hope . . . which often fall short of their good intentions.

I've heard it all before.

"That special someone is just around the corner; you wait and see."

"What about that single over there? To your left—no, your other left. They seem nice!"

"You're such a jewel, I can't understand why you're not married yet."

"It'll be worth the wait, you'll see."

"It'll happen. Don't worry. Just wait."

Don't get me wrong. I'm not saying these statements are wrong or ridiculous. I'm not saying they're not encouraging. I've needed a word of hope many times throughout my years of quagmire-dwelling, and I've been grateful for those who sought to encourage me.

What I *am* saying is that we singles need to understand that most people "out there" don't know what to say to us other than words meant to offer encouragement that looks forward to future happiness. This is largely due to the fact that singles seldom provide anything else for people to comment about in the here and now.

Wait, what?

It's true. Singles, if they must be single, **want** to be acknowledged and respected for the person they are now, not the "lacking individual who hasn't found their better half yet." Unfortunately, however, most singles walk around **acting** like a "lacking individual who hasn't found their better half yet." Their lackluster (or even overwhelmed) approach to life exudes a desire to be married, and screams dissatisfaction with the world until they get what they want (Hmm . . . that kinda sounds like the two-year-old I babysit).

So if you're a single you may be feeling as if nobody knows what to do with you. Advice is empty and repetitive, and life is just one big BLAH!

More than likely . . . you're correct.

So what are you going to do about it?

*What am **I** going to do about it?*

Yes, you! If you feel like any of the above accurately describes your thoughts and feelings, then I want to know how you plan to fix it.

If . . .

- Nobody knows what to do with you, develop personal interests and skills and make them obvious and available to others.
- Advice is empty and repetitive, then heed it, practice it; don't give them a reason to say it again.
- Life is just one big BLAH! Make it an adventure!

Now before you get all annoyed and hoity-toity and look at me like, "So says you!" remember, I'm the one sitting right next to you in the same bog. Same quagmire. Same woeful pit of despondency and absolute rejection that swallows lives whole and leaves pitiful individuals to waste away 'til their unfortunately empty last breath!

Yes, I'm being overdramatic. But I am also still single.

I don't know about you, but I learn best through hands-on experience. And boy, am I getting that! I'm writing this at age 27, still waiting to be married, hoping that God's will for my future includes a family of my own, and still learning to practice what I've been teaching. So after asking how you plan to fix the above problems or misconceptions, I guess it's only fair that I share with you my personal efforts, attempts, failures, and testimony.

My goal with this booklet is not to discourage you or convince you that single life is so much better when you give up all hope of ever getting married. The "singleness book" that had the greatest impact on my life was one that gave the opposite advice: Hope for marriage—prepare for it—but keep *living* even without it. And by living, I mean more than just existing.

So! If you're like me, you probably feel like you keep hearing/reading the same advice over and over, and nothing's helping. I hit that wall last summer. Hard. It hurt. No, really . . . I'll tell ya later.

What I'd like to do now is share with you the concepts, reminders, and words of encouragement that affected me the most. Things that spoke to my heart and actually stuck with me through the years, influencing my life and helping me to the point I'm at now: Still single, still waiting, still hopeful; but also learning to trust, to live, to build. To wait. To be satisfied.

Perhaps nothing in this book will be new to you. Perhaps nothing will impact you to the point where you feel helped. If that's the case, then I hope you at least walk away having shared a laugh with me, or feeling refreshed by the honest and lighthearted perspective I hope to give.

One thing you must remember is that God is not ignoring you. He can hear you crying from the lowest mire just as well as if you were standing on the highest peak of Marital Bliss.

Out of the depths have I cried unto thee, O LORD. Lord, hear my voice: let thine ears be attentive to the voice of my supplications. (Psalm 130:1-2)

Your marital status does not determine how important you are in the sight of God, and your relationship with God is far more important than your marital status.

Before we start, ask the Lord to give you a soft heart toward Him, and to open your eyes to truth. Many times we grow bitter toward Him for keeping us single, and we forget that He longs to have a relationship with us that is far deeper and richer than any we could have on earth. He longs to satisfy you and make you glad.

I have set the LORD always before me: because he is at me right hand, I shall not be moved. Therefore my heart is glad, and my glory rejoiceth: my flesh also shall rest in hope. (Psalm 16:8-9)

Whom have I in heaven but thee? and there is none upon earth that I desire beside thee. (Psalm 73:25)

So let's get started! Plod your way over and sink down for a fun and friendly chat in the mire. Would you care for some coffee or tea? I've got a nice hot cup of Muddy Mocha here just for you . . .

I Just Wanna Be Normal!

I felt like the lowest of human beings. Guilt settled on my eight-year-old shoulders and branded a mark of shame on my heart. I was afraid to look anyone in the eye, sure that they would read my thoughts and gasp in shock.

I had looked at a boy . . . and thought he was cute.

GASP! The horror of such a thought entering someone's head and registering on their impressionable young mind!

I didn't know what to do. I was ashamed that I would think such a thing, and embarrassed to acknowledge the split-second attraction. It felt wrong. It felt scary. But at the same time I wanted to crane my neck around to find the little whippersnapper again.

So I waited until we got home.

I told my mom I needed to tell her something.

And then I cried.[1]

I told my mom about the terrible thought I'd had and waited for her to be shocked, to look sad, to pray that God would forgive me and never allow me to have such thoughts again. I waited for her to be ashamed that a child of hers would go astray as I had done, but she gave me sympathy instead. My mom looked at me with understanding in her eyes as she smiled and spoke words that did wonders to my frantic heart:

"You're normal."

Whether you're still a child of eight or an adult of maturing years, let me encourage you with this simple truth. Attraction is normal. Thinking well about a member of the opposite gender is normal. Further still, it's not a sin!

Let's just face the facts.

To the guys: Girls are pretty.

To the girls: Guys are handsome.

Whew! I'm so relieved somebody said it!

So often we condemn ourselves for noticing when those around us are attractive and nice-looking, we forget to acknowledge that that's the way God made them. He created us after His image, and *He* is perfection and beauty and all goodness. We are allowed to acknowledge that!

So God created man in his own image. In the image of God created he him; male and female created he

---

[1] I was a very emotional child.

> *them. . . . And God saw every thing that he had made, and, behold, it was very good. (Genesis 1:27, 31a)*

> *And the LORD God said, It is not good that the man should be alone; I will make him an help meet for him. . . . And the rib, which the LORD God had taken from man, made he a woman, and brought her unto the man. (Genesis 2:18, 22)*

God made individuals in such a way that we find the other gender attractive. He created within each of us the ability to find both physical and inner beauty in others. <u>Nevertheless, He expects us to bear this gift responsibly</u>.

My mom encouraged me by telling me I'm normal, that my thoughts are normal, and that attraction is not a sin. But she didn't stop there. She also cautioned me.

While the *basic acknowledgement* of someone else's attractiveness is not wrong, what I do with it has the potential to be sinful.

It is not wrong to think someone is nice-looking.

It *is* wrong to think someone is nice-looking, stare, look again, memorize their face, and insert them into today's daydream featuring myself as a blushing bride walking down the aisle to marry the stranger I just crossed paths with at the grocery store. (Girls, don't deny it's happened before. Guys, if you think that's the most ridiculous thing you've ever heard . . . ask for your mother's opinion.)

We are not sinning when we recognize the attractiveness of God's creation, but we are sinning when we dwell on (hold onto, develop, and explore) those thoughts and let them consume us. Holding onto a thought allows it to quickly turn into lust, immoral desires, and impure imaginations or fantasies. It's easy to fall into a pattern of indulging in this kind of thinking because it [temporarily] satisfies our flesh's desire for attention—even if it's all made up and imagined.

Consider this. Thoughts and daydreams take time, and time is precious. As children of God, our time belongs to Him. Would He have you waste it on a passing fancy that will never materialize? Would He have us giving our time to lust and impurity?

Guarding your thought life is not easy. Thoughts come and go so quickly, we often find ourselves wrapped up in a daydream or sinful desire before we realize what hit us, and we have no idea how it got so deep so quick! All through my youth I remember being shocked by thoughts and ideas that managed to infiltrate my mind, to the point I felt dirty.

2 Corinthians 10:3-5 says,

For though we walk in the flesh, we do not war after the flesh: (For the weapons of our warfare are not carnal, but mighty through God to the pulling down of strong holds;) Casting down imaginations, and every high thing that exalteth itself against the knowledge of God, and bringing into captivity every

thought to the obedience of Christ

I had to come to the realization that I was at war. War requires focused effort, intentional drive, and vigilance. Every thought that came into my head had to be examined by the light of truth, and Jesus is truth. I had to take it to Christ. Ask Him to cleanse my mind. And replace the bad with something good.[2]

This is crucial! If you want to get rid of the bad, don't leave room for it to come back or be replaced by something just as vile. Sing a hymn, quote scripture, tell God how much you love Him! The enemy will see that his efforts to destroy you are simply drawing you closer to Christ, and he will have no choice but to retreat.

Learn to say no to impure thoughts. The more you say yes, indulging just once more, the harder it will be to say no when you want out.

How about you? Does the enemy have a strong hold on you? Are you discouraged by thoughts that are impure? Do you feel alone in a world of being helplessly attracted to the opposite gender? Let me encourage you. You're normal. You're not the only one. Others struggle with the same thing. Others have made it through, and so can you.

Don't be afraid to be normal. If you keep yourself wound too tight, afraid even to make eye contact with someone of the opposite gender, you'll fall apart. You'll be discouraged more than not,

---

[2] No matter how unclean, remember that Jesus already knows your thoughts (Psalm 139:1-4). Don't convince yourself that He does not or cannot know the wicked tendencies of your mind.

because you'll constantly fail to meet your own expectations.

Live. Smile. Be a light.

Take your thoughts to Christ—Every. Single. Time.

I readily admit that I still encounter skirmishes in this area, but I can honestly tell you that in my case this battle raged at its most intense for 6 years . . .

The Boat.

My mom says that when you reach the age of 11 or 12 life is like climbing into a boat and starting to row. The waters are a nice ebb and flow, but gradually they get choppy, and then rough, and then all of a sudden you're in a full-blown gale! You're up, you're down, you're going in circles—it's like riding a roller coaster in the dark. In the rain. Alone. And you're crying. Your mom's crying. Your dog's crying. *Everyone's crying!* Then, at long last, everything stops (or at least eases dramatically). The water evens out into a gentle calm and life is suddenly sunny again.[3]

The key to surviving this little boat trip intact is simple. **Give the oars to the Captain.** Keep coming back to Him. Stay close to Him. Keep your eyes and focus on Him. Christ stands ready and willing to steer you safely through the storms of this difficult period of growing up. Don't miss this opportunity to watch Him at work in your life!

Quagmire Keys:
- So. Are you in the boat? Remember that **you're**

---

[3] It's true! I turned 18 and everything was ok! It was a miracle!

normal. Beautifully, blessedly, absolutely normal. And remember that attraction isn't sin; it's what you do with it that defines its role in your life. Don't be afraid of the war you're in. Fight each battle, one at a time. Take each thought to the Lord, stay close to Him, and know that victory is on its way.

Keep thy heart with all diligence; for out of it are the issues of life.
- Proverbs 4:23 -

A Trial is a Trial is a Trial

For years I held my head high. Seated as I was in the depths of the quagmire, I figured if my eyes were up, I wouldn't see it; if my nose was up, I wouldn't smell it. But I could feel it, and deep down I was always aware that it was still there. That I was still there.

My attempt to ignore the mire for the sake of appearances soon began to wear on me. I watched the citizens of Marital Bliss walk by and felt my heart break a little more each time. Trying to pretend that everything was ok was too heavy a burden to carry for so long. I was smiling up at the passersby, but on the inside I was crying.

And then I took a trudge through the sludge, gathered with a number of other girls just like me, and heard someone give a perspective on singleness that I had never considered before:

Singleness is a trial, and it's ok to treat it as such.

All this time I had felt compelled (by society as well as my own pride) to march through life with an attitude that said, "Singleness? Bring it on!" As if proving to the elusive concept of marriage that I was doing just fine without it (when I really wasn't), I kept my head up and laughed off the hopeful encouragement of others.

My real problem was not that I had my head up, but that my eyes were on the wrong thing. They were focused on the mire or the happy borders of Marital Bliss, when they should have been focused on God.

I had categorized singleness as a phase, a time of life, a waiting room or period of in-between. It was something to endure with a brave smile on my face, hoping to reach the other side with that cheerful expression intact. In truth, I saw it as a punishment. To think of singleness as a trial totally stopped me in my tracks. The implications were not only enlightening, they were freeing.

What is a trial?

Webster's 1828 defines **Trial** as Examination and Experience. He says it is *"Examination by a test . . . Experience; suffering that puts strength, patience or faith to the test; afflictions or temptations that exercise and prove the graces or virtues of men."*

Singleness, then, is not a punishment. God is not sitting in heaven laughing at my tears and waiting for me to "get it" or "give up" before He blesses me with what I want. Instead, in spite of me, He is patiently and lovingly wielding this tool called Singleness with a deft and experienced hand, molding and shaping me to be the individual He wants me to be.

I glance around and the quagmire starts to look a little brighter. A little more habitable.

So if I'm going to think of singleness as an experience that tests the strength of my patience and faith in the One who is using it as a tool to mold (and not punish) me, my next question is . . .

How do I face trials?

When I face other, perhaps more obvious trials in my life, what is my response? What do I do to face it? How do I deal with it? And how can I apply those tactics to singleness?

The only way to truly, successfully overcome any trial is to *place it in God's hands and pray for His strength and wisdom to leave it there*. However, many of us, myself included, need ideas and suggestions for how to move on from there. We're still in the middle of a trial, even when we've handed over the reins, so what do we do when our flesh wants to act?

When I'm going through a difficult situation or trying circumstance, I find myself dealing with it both spiritually and physically. Here are some examples:

Spiritually –
- Pray (for myself and others)
- Specifically ask God to handle the situation for me (work it out according to His will)
- Read God's Word (intentionally, even more than usual)
- Sing hymns of <u>praise</u>
- Thank God for every blessing I can think of

Physically –
- Talk about the trial with a mentor/mature Christian
- Surround myself with encouraging/positive people
- Stay active (find a purpose that will distract from the situation and turn your focus outward)
- Help others (meet needs)

What are some other ideas you have? Write your own list of tactics that help you through a trial of any kind:

_____

_____

_____

_____

Now look over our lists once again and apply each suggestion to the concept of facing or dealing with singleness. Are you praying for strength through this trying time? Are you seeking hope and encouragement from God's Word, as well as focusing on developing your walk with Him? Is focus turned outward to the needs of others? Are you praising God in spite of your impatience and discontent?

*By him therefore let us offer the **sacrifice of praise** to God continually, that is, the fruit of our lips giving thanks to his name. (Hebrews 13:15)*

To sacrifice something is "to destroy, surrender [or] devote with loss." So when dealing with a trial we ought to . . .

- **Destroy** words of complaint by offering thanks instead,
- **Surrender** your will by thanking God for His, and
- **Devote with loss**—give God the glory, honor, and praise, no matter how much it pains you to accept and acknowledge that His way is indeed perfect and best.

Facing a trial honestly—for what it is—creates room for hope. Mankind sees a trial as something to push through and overcome. It is something God uses to make us better. We see it as a season, regardless of how long it may last, and somewhere in the back of our minds is the truth that all seasons come to an end.

Therefore! If singleness is a trial, we can have hope that
1. It can be conquered/overcome,
2. It will eventually come to an end, and
3. God is able to grow us as individuals and make us better and stronger through the experience.

Remember, God would not lead you into this time of testing if He knew you could not make it out. He does not give us burdens that are too heavy for us to bear with His aid. Have you asked for His help in bearing this load? In seeing you through this trial? In giving you grace to accept it and work through it? In helping you to learn and grow through it?

Cast thy burden upon the LORD, and he shall sustain thee: he shall never suffer the righteous to be moved. (Psalm 55:22)

Be merciful unto me, O God, be merciful unto me: for my soul trusteth in thee: yea, in the shadow of thy wings will I make my refuge, until these calamities be overpast. (Psalm 57:1)

Why so lonely?

Another thing to keep in mind as you take a look at the trial of singleness is that you're not the only one!

There hath no temptation taken you but such as is common to man: but God is faithful, who will not suffer you to be tempted above that ye are able; but will with the temptation also make a way to escape, that ye may be able to bear it. (1 Corinthians 10:13)

We need to be careful that we don't get so wrapped up in ourselves that we forget others around us are experiencing the same struggles, hardships, and feelings of hopelessness. There are many singles around you who are sitting in the same pit of sticky despair, trying to ignore the mire and hoping that it will simply disappear if they ignore or endure it long enough.

If you start to feel sorry for yourself because you've *waited so loooooooooooong*, then take a good look around you. You're bound to discover someone who's waited longer than you (for a spouse, a baby, a house, a job . . .).

If you start to feel sorry for yourself because that burden of being alone is so heavy and unbearable, then take a good look around. You're bound to discover someone who is feeling alone, not because they haven't found that special someone, but because they *lost* that special someone (or a parent, a child, a house, a job . . .).

Singleness is not the only trial you will face in life. Learn to face it—to deal with it—now. Seek the Lord and His strength today so that this response will be more natural when you meet a new trial tomorrow.

In closing this section let me remind you that trials tend to produce a line of thinking that is unclear and distorted (due to emotional overdrive and fatigue; whether physical, spiritual, or mental). When this happens we must "argue" with ourselves and continually point our thoughts toward truth. Even simple truths such as "God is good," or "God loves me and wants what's best for me," and reminders such as "If it's God's will that I marry, then it will happen not a moment sooner or later than He has planned" will eventually break through and encourage the heart.

If you tell yourself something often enough, you will eventually believe it. What better to believe than the truth?

Quagmire Keys:
- **Don't be afraid to view singleness as a trial.** Facing it openly and honestly allows room for hope as we find untried ways to deal with the experience and its effect on our life. Sharing the load/burden/hardship with God makes it easier, for He is ready and willing to carry it for us.
- Remember, a trial is not something to be merely endured; it is to be conquered, and it is an experience used by God to shape us into better individuals.

Seek the LORD and his strength, seek his face continually. (1 Chronicles 16:11)

Seek the LORD, and his strength: seek his face evermore. (Psalm 105:4)

Come unto me, all ye that labour and are heavy laden, and I will give you rest. Take my yoke upon you, and learn of me; for I am meek and lowly in heart: and ye shall find rest unto your souls. For my yoke is easy, and my burden is light.
- Matthew 11:28-30 -

Idol Desires

Now that we've looked at singleness as a trial, and seen it as something that affects us from the outside, it's time to acknowledge and discuss a truth from the inside. This one digs a little deeper and may be a little painful.

Singleness is not your "fault," but the discontentment and bitterness and resentment you have towards being single . . . is.

Perhaps you feel like you've accepted your place in the quagmire. You're resigned to a fate of eternal sludge-sitting, and are determined to face each new day with a battle-ready countenance, ready to deal with this trial in bravery.

And yet . . . every time your gaze rests on the merry inhabitants of Marital Bliss; every time your mailbox spills out glaring requests to "Save the Date!"; every time you scroll through the 1,753 notifications declaring that all of your friends are in a relationship, engaged, walking down the aisle, or pregnant . . .

You're not really feelin' the love for your little place in the mud.

In fact, you hate it.

I speak to myself first of all. I can't tell you how many times I've clicked that little "Login" button only to roll my eyes and wonder why I put myself through the agony. The majority of my friends who were married years ago are now having their second or third child, and I can only watch as the next wave of engagements roles in.

And a lot of them are my younger sister's friends.

Ooooohhh, it's *discouraging!*

I repeated this process over and over before I came to realize I was having trouble fulfilling the will of God in Romans 12:15 that says,

Rejoice with them that do rejoice, and weep with them the weep.

I was weeping, but it was all for me. I couldn't smile for, exclaim over, or be happy about, all the wonderful things that were happening in lives of my friends, because I was too busy coveting those events for myself.

I had to ask myself, do I want my friends to rejoice with me when the time comes? Why would they? Why should they? What kind of reaction will I receive if I reap the kind of congratulations I have sown?

These questions started me on a journey to discover what was really going on in my heart. What was the reason behind my inability to rejoice? Why would a reminder of my own singleness produce thoughts that were bitter and resentful? And who or what was I really resenting? The happy bride and groom . . . or the God who had brought them together?

In searching for these answers I was constantly brought back to the same suggestion. Conferences, books, sermons, parental guidance, and the examination of my own heart, all pointed to the conclusion that marriage was my idol.

I had always recoiled from this concept. Of course I loved God better than anything and anyone! I would never idolize anything!

And then God brought me to face a fact and answer a question, which, when combined, exposed the ugly truth so that I could not possibly ignore or deny it.

The fact: An idol is anything I love more than God; anything that usurps His place in my life.

Naturally I argued that there was nothing I loved more than God. I knew His rightful place, and I would never give that place to anything or anyone else.

I was lying to myself. And this was exposed when I was struck by a very clear, very direct, very revealing question.

The question: If Jesus returned today—*while you are still single*—to take His children to be with Him in glory, would you be happy about it?

Now, I understand that in reality when we reach heaven we'll be overwhelmed by the glory and majesty of God, and we won't be worrying about whether or not we got married back on earth. But just for a moment, think with me in theory. If you knew Jesus Christ was coming today, and you would be leaving this earth as a single, would you be ok with that?

What is your first and honest reaction?

Maybe the thought fills your heart with joy. Maybe you can honestly look heavenward and cry out, "Come quickly, Lord Jesus!" Not me. I was not ok with that thought. Shamefully, I had to acknowledge that I would rather the Lord delay His coming so that I could experience this greatest and deepest desire of my heart. So that I could have what I wanted.

Several things were revealed by this realization:
1. I loved the idea of marriage more than I loved God; which meant that
2. My relationship with Christ was not as strong and vibrant as it should be; also
3. I was indeed harboring an idol in my heart, which is the temple of God; and
4. I had not truly surrendered my desires to God. I was still setting my wants and my way above His.

In spite of coming to these realizations and beginning to understand the terrible condition that my heart was in I continued to largely ignore the real issue and root problems, and instead tried to overcome the surface-level results on my own. It was like trying to eliminate the entire quagmire of singleness by scooping out a few cups of the mire and calling it progress.

It was not until last summer that God finally gripped my heart and brought me to my knees . . .

Embedded Desire

My bitterness toward God over my continued singleness was producing bitter fruit that grew harder and harder to ignore or overcome. Minor struggles with fleshly thoughts and desires were an everyday occurrence. My emotions crowded just beneath the surface, and frustration was a constant companion. I was sarcastic whenever the subject of marriage was raised. Contentment was officially elusive.[4]

As an author I was serving the Lord through my writing, but hoping with each completed publication that *now* God would send my spouse. I was trying to satisfy God while refusing to remove the idol that stood in His place.

Outwardly, my life looked like one of spiritual victory as I learned to wear the façade of a joyful single. Inwardly, the throne-room of my heart was in disarray as I became consumed with indulging my greatest desire and trying to control its building unrest. The dangerous fact was that I remained this way for so long I convinced myself that I was truly content, and that my hardships were a result of the enemy attacking my joy. I believed I was right where God wanted me.

In the summer of 2015 I was planning to attend a Single Ladies' Retreat with my mom and two of my sisters. We had been to this particular conference before, and I figured everything that was going to be said would be a repeat of everything I'd heard before. So I would go for the fellowship, and hope for some refreshing encouragement.

In the weeks before the retreat the ladies

---

[4] Not to be mistaken with "illusive."

planning the event sent out a list of prayer requests regarding the details for the weekend, including hearts that would be softened toward the voice of God. That was a request I tackled with diligence. After all, I was content with being single and wanted other young ladies to reach that same place of "sold-out" joy.

Mmhmm . . .

So I prayed. I asked God to soften and prepare the hearts of the women planning to attend, and to make them ready for the teaching they would hear.

I didn't really include myself in that prayer because I didn't think God could reach my heart any more than He already had. I mean, I was fine—I was content! But God included me anyway. He knew without my saying so that my heart was in desperate need of renovation.

In the days that followed, my battle for contentment became fierce. God would knock on the walls of my heart, reminding me He was there, and with every gentle tap the balance of my world was shaken. Every day brought hardship as I dealt with the same struggles I had overcome a thousand times before. I was tired. I was grasping for a sense of peace, angered by the mere thought of being single, and doubting that God was truly working all things together for my good.[5]

Finally . . . it happened.

The crisis. The moment of truth.

I hit a wall. An insurmountable wall of discouragement.

I was having a conversation with my mom, being

---

[5] Romans 8:25-28

a grouch and having a hard time keeping bitterness out of my voice. Eventually I broke down and started to cry (still angry), and sulked off to my room to have a pity party. When I got to the "party" however, the only other guest in attendance was God, and He wasn't there to let me sulk. He gave my heart one last soul-stirring knock and I fell to my knees.

Now I was really crying. Sobbing.

I knew what He wanted.

And I didn't want to give it to Him.

"Lord," I wept, "this dream, this desire to be married and to have children, has been my dearest . . . my deepest. I have clung to this, longed for this, desired this for so long, and so deeply, that to extract it would be painful. It has become such a part of me, engraved into who I am. I don't want to let go."

I had tried before to give my desire to God, but always with this thought in the back of my mind that He would still fulfill it. I would give Him my desire to be married, but remind myself that God was still able to make it happen.

This time . . . He wanted the whole thing.

Of course, deep down I understood that His will would ultimately be done, but I knew without a doubt that this time—in this moment—God wanted me to ignore that. To give Him the desire without acknowledging His ability to give it back. He wanted total surrender, and I knew He was going to have to take it because in my own strength I was unable to deliver.

I prayed that He would make me willing to live without my desire, and that He would give me strength. I prayed for the willingness of Abraham, who had total belief that God would provide that joy *another way*—that God would satisfy and fulfill His promises, even if it was through a different outlet than expected.

> *And Abraham said, My son, God will provide himself a lamb for a burnt offering: so they went both of them together. . . . And Abraham lifted up his eyes, and looked, and behold behind him a ram caught in a thicket by his horns: and Abraham went and took the ram, and offered him up for a burnt offering in the stead of his son. (Genesis 22:8, 13)*

There were several promises that God had given to me over the years, and reflecting on them at this point helped to shift my perspective. I started to see how petty my complaints were, and how much bigger God was in the grand scheme of things than I had been giving Him credit for. How could I be discontent with my Saviour? The God of the universe!

I asked God to show me His love, and to let me see evidence of that love every day. I asked for His forgiveness. I had harbored bitterness toward Him when I couldn't have my way, and I had resented His perfect plan. I thanked Him for giving me work to do through my writing and asked for continued strength to serve and bring Him glory in that way.

I also prayed scripture. "Help me to go in the strength of the Lord God; serving You in all humility of mind, tasting and seeing that You are good. Let

God be magnified."[6]

The Bible says in Psalm 16:11

> *Thou wilt show me the path of life: in thy presence is fulness of joy; at thy right hand there are pleasures for evermore.*

The longer I spent in the presence of God, the larger-than-life I found Him to be, and the smaller and insignificant I saw myself. God was in control (even when I pretended that I was), and that was how it should be. This was where I could rest, knowing that He holds all my hopes in His hands and that He has the power to make everything new.

I came away from that time on my knees with one phrase ringing in my head:

> *Satisfied with Christ.*

I don't mean for this to come across like some mystical repetition deal, or even a self-motivation pump talk. It was and is a *reminder*. Relief was instant, but victory was ongoing. To this day I still encounter struggles or thoughts of discontent, and I find that to simply take a minute to remind myself who is in control—that I can be *satisfied with Christ*—helps me to refocus on God and remember Who the big picture is really about.

---

[6] Psalm 71:16, Acts 20:19, Psalm 34:8, Psalm 70:4

*As for me, I will behold thy face in righteousness: I shall be **satisfied**, when I awake, **with thy likeness**. (Psalm 17:15)*

Head Knowledge vs. Heart Wisdom

The ladies' retreat that summer was more than refreshing. Yes, I heard many things that I had heard before, but this time my heart was ready. Having God speak to my heart the week before made hearing the same thing over and over a matter of confirmation and encouragement. It solidified what God had spoken to my heart, and grew upward from heart to head in a way that was easier to accept and comprehend due to experience.

- **Head knowledge** tries to penetrate from head to heart. It may sound good, but it won't be able to take root in a heart of prejudiced stone.
- **Heart wisdom** springs up and flows outward. It is [head] knowledge with a foundation. It has first taken root and will therefore be stronger and surer.

Now don't get me wrong. Don't read this section and believe for a minute that I no longer desired to be married. As I moved forward from that day I did still desire to be married, but this was balanced by contentment. I was given a picture to illustrate this, and it completed this time of teaching that God had brought me through.

During my prayer, I spoke to God about the idea that my desire for marriage had become so embedded in my heart that to take it out would be painful. It was a part of me, and I couldn't extract it without causing damage and a great amount of anguish. I'm sure God could have done so if He wished, but instead He comforted me with a realization.

He didn't want me to take it out.

Wait a minute . . . All that sacrifice and all those tears were unnecessary?!?

Not at all! The sacrifice and tears brought me to a place where I focused on God instead of myself, and created a desire to be satisfied with Christ (whether or not I was married).

In my mind I could see the image of a heart, and wrapped around it were a number of tangled vines. The vines were embedded, and their ends had dug deep into the heart.

Imagine the damage you would cause the heart if you tried to uproot and rip out the vines!

This was my argument before God, but I quickly discovered that I had spoken too soon. He didn't want me to tear out the "vines" . . . He wanted access to them. He wanted to be the source of life that flowed through them.

I am the vine, ye are the branches: He that abideth in me, and I in him, the same bringeth forth much fruit: for without me ye can do nothing. (John 15:5)

What would happen if I placed my desire in God's hands and let Him flow through it? What if I let Him fill my heart with His desires? Change my plans to reflect His own?

Psalm 37: 4 says,

Delight thyself also in the LORD: and he shall give

thee the desires of thine heart.

That doesn't mean He'll give me anything I desire (*verb*), but rather He'll give me the desire (*noun*) itself. And if God is the one Who causes you to desire something, you can trust that He plans to make it happen!

Quagmire Keys:
- Examine your heart for the presence of an idol. Is there anything you love more than God? Do you desire a spouse more than you desire to know God? What are your thoughts when you consider that Jesus may very well return while you're still single?
- Are you **satisfied with Christ**?
- An embedded desire out of control is an idol at home in your heart.

Whom have I in heaven but thee? and there is none upon earth that I desire beside thee. My flesh and my heart faileth: but God is the strength of my heart, and my portion for ever.
- Psalm 73:25-26 -

Making the While Worthwhile

If you've ever read a book, heard a seminar, or watched a documentary about singleness, I'm sure you've been introduced to the concept of redeeming the time. As unmarrieds we are exhorted not to waste our single years. This is a time we will never get back, when we have the opportunity to accomplish things that may not be possible in the years to come. During this time, if you are still living at home, you do not bear the responsibilities that come with a place of your own, and you have fewer obligations.

The world will tell you to live it up, and enjoy the freedom while it lasts. Break the rules and do your own thing now, before it's time to settle down and behave.

I would like to encourage you to live, and not simply exist, but to use the rules and structure you've learned before now to propel you forward and act as the foundation for your future. If you want to examine what you believe because you're not certain what you believe for yourself, then find out! But, please! Do so from a point of safety.

You were raised a certain way for specific reasons. As you reach adulthood and start making decisions for yourself, there's no reason to jump overboard to test the waters through immersion. You can see and study the water from where you are; you can observe the consequences of jumping in without doing so yourself, and you can also turn around and study the place you're at in an up-close and detailed way.

If you want to know what you believe, then start by studying what you were taught and why you were taught it. Chances are, you'll gain an even greater appreciation for your upbringing.

Christians are expected to live in a way that pleases God, and unbelievers are often more attune to an erring Christian than we are. The time we have is precious, and singleness is not an excuse to waste it on any number of fun-seeking blunders.

See then that ye walk circumspectly, not as fools, but as wise, Redeeming the time, because the days are evil. (Ephesians 5:15-16)

Anyway! Back to our discussion . . .

Yes, use this time to accomplish things that may be harder to get done later, but make sure your focus is right. God gave you a unique set of skills and abilities so that you could use those talents to serve

Him and bring Him glory. That is what this time of singleness is for!

Cultivate now the characteristics that will define you later!

I'm not saying that someone who marries young (has fewer single years) will be a bland, undefined, character-less individual. I am saying that someone who remains single longer obviously has more time to sharpen their focus on what is truly important, and to gain a solid footing on who they are in Christ without the *added* influences and expectations that come with married life.

Start by making a list of all the talents, abilities, and skills that God has given you, and then list the various avenues or outlets that are available to you for developing and putting into practice those abilities.

How can you use them to serve God?

Personally, I had a love for storytelling and a desire for wholesome reading material that was safe for my younger siblings to read. So I started writing books that don't really fit into any one genre due to their wide-range audience and a mixture of faith and clean fantasy, and I determined to weave godly principles and character traits, as well as the Gospel, into the fabric of each story.

I also love children and had a desire to care for them. I've been amazed to watch God open door after door of opportunity, keeping me in the babysitting business for seven years now! Throughout this time I've been able to cultivate skills that will be useful for my future as I learned to care for a home and the little people who live there.[7]

Depending on your own interests, writing books or babysitting may sound absolutely boring, unimpressive, or positively terrifying; but God has used the process to enrich my life in the same way He can take your skills and use them to grow you.

Webster says that to redeem time *"is to use more diligence in the improvement of it; to be diligent and active in duty and preparation."* Your **duty** as a child of God is to **diligently** use your time wisely and for His glory, and also to **prepare** for whatever future He has for you by keeping your personal or individual skills **active** to prevent them from rusting or going to waste.

So make this time count by "cashing in" and claiming God's best in return!

Woes & Whoas

There are some things about singleness that we think about with an attitude of *woe* that actually deserve a heartfelt *whoa!* For instance . . .

---

[7] Remember what we talked about *waaaaay* back in the introduction? "Hope for marriage—prepare for it—but keep *living* even without it." Preparing to run a home of my own isn't wrong, but becoming angry and bitter when I don't get that home in *my timing* would be.

Woe	*Whoa!*
"I'm in a state of social limbo. I'm no longer a young adult, but I'm not married yet, so I don't fit in with the adults either!"	An adult single has the maturity to converse with an older crowd, and yet still has the ability to relate to young adults in a way a married person may not. They have the freedom to mingle in multiple groups without expectations.
"I don't have a spouse!"	A single has the ability to hop up and go, or make plans without needing to consult the schedule or bank account of their spouse (i.e. Over the past few years I've been able to do a lot of traveling and vacationing with friends that wouldn't have been possible if I'd been married).

What are some other areas you can think of? Consider all the aspects of singleness that you find negative, and search for a positive aspect. It's gotta be there somewhere!

Quagmire Keys:
- Singleness is a time of opportunity. Make it a time

you can look back on with a smile by using it to **serve the Lord and cultivate godly character**!
- Find the positive aspects of your life, and adjust your attitude toward singleness to one of ***Whoa!*** instead of one of *woe.*

Walk in wisdom toward them that are without, redeeming the time.

- Colossians 4:5 -

Joseph & Asenath
A Story of Great Expectations

I thought I'd be married at the age of eighteen.
Honestly.
I know some girls say that even though it's glaringly obvious they're not ready at all, but I really *really* thought I would marry young. And I really *really* thought I was ready.

I reached eighteen and my days were made of anticipation. I hadn't mastered every life skill, but I was willing to learn on the job (especially since I learn best through experience, so things were looking up).

The anticipation soared.
I turned nineteen.
The anticipation dragged.
Now, fast forward nine years from my age of expectation and I'm sitting at my desk writing a booklet about **STILL** being single, and hoping to somehow someway offer a bit of encouragement to

those of you who are sitting beside me in this cheerless bog of despondency.

Cue sad violin music

Pass the tissues, will you? And the coffee—my Muddy Mocha's getting cold.

Time is passing! I'm getting old! I'm no longer just a *single*, now I'm an *older single!!*

All that aside, the truth is that it's taken me all these years to finally realize and admit . . .

I wasn't ready.

True, I still believe that I *could* have married at eighteen; I could have survived, learned, and even had a good marriage. My problem was that I wasn't ready spiritually. I didn't know how to be satisfied with Christ (something I'm still learning), or how to sacrifice my expectations. And if I can't learn these things as a single, it will be harder to learn them when I'm married.

Let me be clear. I'm not saying I had to learn these lessons before God could bless me with a spouse. It simply would have been harder to learn later.

I dislike the concept that God is waiting for you to surrender your desire for marriage before He will bless you with it. If God wills it, you will marry not a moment sooner or later than you're meant to. There is nothing you can do to either stop it or hurry it along! Our problem is that we want that moment to come according to *our* timetable, and we don't like to think that His timetable is different and that single is what we need to be for now.

In our first section (*I Just Wanna Be Normal!*) I spoke particularly to younger singles. I'd like to finish up by sharing several observations that have spoken to my heart as a single in my late-twenties.

By the start of 2016 I was at a place in life where I was feeling "old." I *knew all the right answers* when it came to singleness, waiting, God's timing and will being perfect, etc., and I believed them. But I'm still human, and occasionally I still experience a devastating fear that by the time I marry, it will be too late for me to have children and raise a family. Again, I know the truthful responses to these thoughts, and that God is not the author of fear,[8] but sometimes I let fear work a debilitating number on my mind and all reason goes out the window.

In January our assistant pastor preached a sermon and while I couldn't tell you, months later, what the rest was about, it was the last ten minutes—a final point that he "just added in"—that struck a chord in my heart and gave me a whole new perspective on being an older single.

Joseph

In the biblical account of Joseph[9] we can't say for sure what Joseph expected for his life, but I have to believe it wasn't slavery. If he was like the other young men of his day, perhaps he expected to inherit from his father (as the favorite son) and to marry and raise a family of his own.

Then his brothers sell him as a slave, and he is ultimately thrown into prison for a crime he did not commit. He spent years in prison. Time was passing, and he was tucked out of sight from the world, and I think we can safely say that marriage prospects were

---

[8] 2 Timothy 1:7
[9] Genesis 37-50

pretty slim. Okay, nonexistent.

Throughout these difficult years of trial and temptation, however, Joseph maintained his integrity and character, fought for his purity, and his life was marked by constant victory and favor.

> *And the LORD was with Joseph, and he was a prosperous man . . . And Joseph was a goodly person, and well favoured. (Genesis 39:2, 6)* [10]

Then comes the day when Joseph is brought before Pharaoh to interpret a dream. His services earn his freedom, but remember, he's no longer a young teen or even in his early twenties:

> *And Joseph was thirty years old when he stood before Pharaoh king of Egypt. (Genesis 41:46a)*

It would not be far-fetched to imagine that Joseph had lost hope (or given up his expectation) to be married. He had lived as a slave, spent years in prison, and was now set to serve at Pharaoh's bidding. Nevertheless, in the end [as a reward?] God gave him Asenath.

> *And Pharaoh . . . gave [Joseph] to wife Asenath the daughter of Potipherah priest of On. (Genesis 41:45)*

---

[10] See also Genesis 39:2-6, 20-23; 41:38-44;

And unto Joseph were born two sons before the years of famine came, which Asenath the daughter of Potipherah priest of On bare unto him. (Genesis 41:50)

How about that!? Not only did God bless Joseph with a wife, He also gave them a family!

Now at this point, as a girl (guys, bear with me, this is for you too), I have to think of Asenath. Of course this is speculation, but living as she did in an era when people commonly married very young, and being the daughter of a respected man (a priest in Egypt), I wonder if Asenath had lost hope.

The Bible doesn't give her age, but just imagining her scenario as similar to my own was thought provoking. She was obviously a suitable choice for Joseph. What if she was in her late-twenties?

Imagine her wonder when, in God's timing—and when Joseph would most appreciate the miracle—she became Joseph's reward! All those years of turmoil, hardship, and trial, were at last crowned by the unexpected blessing of marriage, and she was the bride!

So my thought is . . . Coming into my late-twenties, with no "prospects" on the horizon, what if God is keeping me for a Joseph?

Girls, what if God is saving you—setting you apart—to be some Joseph's reward?

Guys, what if God has plans for your life that are best fulfilled without the responsibility of a family, and He is ready and waiting to reward you with an Asenath?

Are you willing to wait? Patiently?

Are you willing to redeem the time, and make the wait worthwhile?

And therefore will the LORD wait, that he may be gracious unto you, and therefore will he be exalted, that he may have mercy upon you: for the LORD is a God of judgment: blessed are all they that wait for him. (Isaiah 30:18)

This verse really came alive for me when I adjusted my view of the word "judgment." I tend to skim over that word, applying it generally as the judge-passing-a-verdict kind of judgment. Take a minute to re-read it, and when you come to that part, think of the making-good-and-sound-choices kind of judgment . . .

If God makes us wait, it is because He is gracious, and we can be sure He is doing us a favor.

I can wait for His timing because I can trust His *judgment.*

And I will be blessed for trusting His judgment because that is when I'm resting in His grace.

So maybe you're still harboring great expectations for a spouse and family of your own. Just remember . . .

God has great expectations for you

and His timetable may look different than yours. Understand, when I talk about God's expectations

I'm not talking about the *will of God* for your life, which *will* be performed. I'm using this phrase to define all the opportunities He makes available for you to redeem this time of singleness by serving Him with your time and talents.

For we are his workmanship, created in Christ Jesus unto good works, which God hath before ordained that we should walk in them. (Ephesians 2:10)

You have the choice to accept or deny those opportunities. You will either remain waist-deep in the quagmire, waiting to be pulled out . . .

Or you will do something to make your time in the bog worthwhile.

If God has not brought you a spouse yet, then it's time to accept that it's just not time yet! And that means you can trust that, like Joseph, you're right in the middle of exploring, understanding, and living out God's expectations for you.

And that, my friend, is an exciting place to be.

Quagmire Keys:
- Just because you have the perfect preconceived plan for your life doesn't mean it's the best option. **God has expectations for your life**; are you willing to lose yours in order to fully experience His?
- Remember the story of Joseph and his single years. **Be a treasure worth the wait, and be willing to wait for a treasure**.

My soul, wait thou only upon God; for my expectation is from him.
- Psalm 62:5 -

In Closing
Build Up, Rise Up

*S*o, you say, as you motion with your mug of Muddy Mocha, *we've made it to the end of this thing, and . . . we're still sitting in the bog.*

This book is not and was not meant to be an extensive study on all things single. There are so many related topics we could have discussed at length (purity; living at home; common influences that encourage discontent; etc.), but if we had this wouldn't be a booklet, but a gargantuan tome most likely relegated to the mundane job of a doorstop.

My desire was to simply outline several points that were especially meaningful for me, in hopes that they would also encourage you. My hope is that you will be able to go back now and at least begin to answer that question from our introduction: *If nobody knows what to do with you, advice is empty and repetitive, and life is just one big BLAH! What are you going to do about it?*

Perhaps you've already heard everything in this book before. Maybe you weren't helped at all, but instead you're even more confused (*Why are we sitting in a bog, anyway?*). Perhaps you've already reached that place of contentment and satisfaction in Christ, and you just wanted another perspective, or the encouraging realization that you're not the only one who struggles in this area. Because it is an ongoing struggle! If you're content today, chances are you'll be struggling tomorrow, but don't give up! God may allow a struggle to arise in order to point your focus back to Him.

May each struggle bring you back to being satisfied with Christ!

I believe perfect contentment will only be achieved when we reach Heaven; but I also believe that with God's help we can experience a taste of it here on earth.

Whatever the case, I hope you've come to realize that desiring marriage is not a bad thing. You're allowed to hope for it, prepare for it, and even wait for it. But in your hoping, long for God's best. In your preparation, serve the Lord. And in your waiting, trust His judgment.

Yea, in the way of thy judgments, O LORD, have we waited for thee; the desire of our soul is to thy name, and to the remembrance of thee.
- Isaiah 26:8 -

Sitting here, twiddling my thumbs in the mud that surrounds me, I look around and start to realize that others have begun to pull planks of wood from the banks. Those well-intentioned individuals who dwell in Marital Bliss help by passing the harder-to-reach pieces. Singles take a plank and hand one to their sinking neighbor with a smile (actually making eye-contact and surviving! *Gasp!*). I watch, curious, until someone passes a piece to me.

"What do I do with it?" I ask, totally confused.

"Build upward." They reply. Their smile encourages, and their words inspire a sense of hope. I look around at the singles who surround me, some using the planks while others stare at the wood with disgust and disillusionment.

"What am I supposed to build?"

Someone passing by on the bank looks down at me, "What are you able to build? What needs are you capable of meeting?" They hand me another plank and move on.

I set the piece of wood flat on top of the mire and realize that it stays afloat. There's a promising start. I take the other piece and lay it beside the first, connecting the two to create a wider platform.

All around me I hear the efforts of others as they build their own platforms, some digging deep to anchor their handiwork in the floor of the bog. I collect pieces of wood and continue to connect the pieces as I'm able until I look up and see that a small hut has taken shape, with the original platform serving as a base.

With excitement I pull myself up out of the quagmire and sit beneath the roof of my hut. Here is a place I can live and work above the mud and mire.

Here I can dwell and work until the day I'm called to cross over to the banks of Marital Bliss. From here I can better see the flowers, the meadows, the mountains in the distance. I look forward to a time when I may live there, but for now I'm able to enjoy the beauty of the surrounding land as never before.

My altered position has given me a new and fresh perspective.

And now I set to work. Within the safety (and dryness) of my hut I write stories to share with others. I care for children whose parents walk along the banks, and I'm greatly rewarded by the love that they give me in return.

I can't help but smile as I experience this new joy, this unexplainable relief that comes from trying to make my time in this place worthwhile. All around me I see huts and stands of different shapes, sizes, and purpose. Each one reflects and functions according to the interests, skills, and abilities of the builder.

And now, with anticipation I wonder . . .

What will you build?

About the Author

Nicole Sager is a homeschool graduate and an avid reader. She lives with her wonderful parents and has five awesome siblings. Nicole enjoys a number of hobbies, but especially reading and writing (and always with a cup of coffee).

"In writing each book, I pray that it will bring honor and glory to God, and that He will use it as a tool to bring at least one person to the saving knowledge of Jesus Christ. I pray that my books would be a blessing to readers (individuals & families alike) as they search for wholesome yet exciting reading material for all ages."

- Nicole

Author Fun Fact!
So far Nicole has spent 7 of her **bog**-sitting years **baby**sitting 9 children from 4 different families!

www.facebook.com/arcreabooks
www.pinterest.com/heartofarcrea
www.arcreabooks.wix.com/nicole-sager

CPSIA information can be obtained
at www.ICGtesting.com
Printed in the USA
LVHW080206240121
677278LV00050B/1663